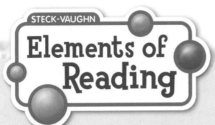

STECK-VAUGHN
Elements of Reading

P9-DGE-561

Vocabulary

Isabel L. Beck, Ph.D., and Margaret G. McKeown, Ph.D.

Writer's Log

Illustrations
Amy Wummer

Photography
Additional photography by PhotoDisc/Getty Images, Bob Masheris, Corbis Royalty Free, Victoria Smith, Art Parts, Comstock, Benone de Lima, Dynamic Graphics.

Steck Vaughn™
A Harcourt Achieve Imprint

www.Steck-Vaughn.com
1-800-531-5015

ISBN 1-4190-3048-5

Copyright © 2007 Harcourt Achieve Inc.

Printed in China 6 7 8 9 10 0940 12 11 10 09

Hello!

This Writer's Log is a place for you to use some new and exciting words in your writing. Some of the words might be a challenge to learn. But once you learn them, they will help you say exactly what you mean!

Now, let the writing begin!

CONTENTS

Take It Further

triumph	Something that is a triumph is a great success or achievement.

The school cookie sale was a triumph because

divine	If you call something divine, you are saying it is so wonderful it seems to come from out of this world.

Sheila thought her dress was divine because

dazzle	Something that dazzles you is so bright or so beautiful that it makes it hard to see.

Looking out my window, I was dazzled by

vanish	If someone or something vanishes, they disappear suddenly in a way that can't be explained.

Paul made the cookie vanish when

| stupefy | If something stupefies you, it surprises you so much that it's hard to think. |

Opening the door to my room, I was stupefied by

| crave | If you crave something, you want it so much you can hardly think of anything else. |

My stomach was full after dinner, but Gretchen still craved

| dejected | When you are dejected, you feel sad because you've been disappointed by something. |

I felt dejected at the end of the day because

| fulfill | When a wish, dream, or hope is fulfilled, it comes true. |

Arturo's mother fulfilled his wish when

- [ ] **triumph**
- [ ] **divine**
- [ ] **dazzle**
- [ ] **vanish**
- [ ] **stupefy**
- [ ] **crave**
- [ ] **dejected**
- [ ] **fulfill**

How Many Words Can I Use?

And still make sense!

Write about what you read in "Escape the Ordinary." Did you like the story about the king and the jester? Pretend you were the king. What would you have done to the jester?

VOCABULARY JUMBLE

The vocabulary word that best fits each clue is hidden in the jumbled letters. Find the word and connect the letters. The first one has been done for you.

dazzle
dejected
triumph

stupefy
crave

fulfill
vanish
divine

N	P	E	D
D	I	L	S
E	V	I	O
R	C	N	E

1. Great dessert, Kevin! The chocolate sauce was simply _____!

L	O	F	R
L	S	U	G
I	F	L	J
M	E	A	R

2. Tina thinks that if she had enough money, she could _____ all of her dreams.

S	T	H	Q
L	I	S	V
A	N	E	P
V	R	M	O

3. I was so embarrassed after falling down, I wished I could just _____.

L	A	M	T
B	S	R	T
V	R	A	V
Y	C	L	E

4. Josh always does silly things to interrupt class. He must _____ attention.

W	H	P	M
M	Z	T	U
A	P	R	I
S	T	L	Q

5. I thought our cat walking business would be a _____, but no one hired us.

A	D	P	Y
Z	V	F	Z
Z	L	E	O
S	R	R	D

6. The full moon and bright stars _____ the eyes, don't they?

S	T	L	Y
P	U	B	F
E	M	H	P
F	Y	U	O

7. I know I'll _____ the audience when I play the flute with my nose.

O	D	E	R
J	R	T	C
E	M	D	E
S	C	E	J

8. She must feel _____ after not winning a prize in the science fair.

In My Own Words

Check the prompt that you want to write about. Then write a story using as many of the vocabulary words as possible. Have fun, but make sense!

☐ Think about a time when you were completely surprised by something. What happened? What did you do? What did you say?

☐ Think about a time when you succeeded at something you didn't expect to succeed at doing. How did you feel? Did you celebrate? Write a poem about your success.

☐ Think of your own story and write about it.

Take It Further

cubicle	A cubicle is a small, enclosed space that is used for a particular activity.

My bedroom is really more like a cubicle, because

bail	If you bail out of a situation, you get out of it because it is getting difficult or dangerous.

We had to bail out of our hiking trip because

reinforce	If you reinforce something, you add something else to it to make it stronger or harder.

When the mice started getting into our food, we reinforced the cabinet doors by

expel	To expel something means to force it out.

We had to expel the cat from the house because

| abandon | Abandoning something means leaving it behind when you don't want to or should not. |

Ben abandoned his bicycle even though

| impetuous | Someone who is impetuous does things quickly, without thought or care. |

Danica acted impetuously when

| dilemma | A dilemma is a situation without an easy solution, usually because all the choices are equally good or equally bad. |

Yesterday I had quite a dilemma on my hands when

| resolutely | If you do something resolutely, you do it without changing your mind or giving up. |

She worked resolutely on her difficult math homework because

- ☐ cubicle
- ☐ bail
- ☐ reinforce
- ☐ expel
- ☐ abandon
- ☐ impetuous
- ☐ dilemma
- ☐ resolutely

How Many Words Can I Use?

And still make sense!

Write about what you read in "Taking the Plunge." Did you think the puffin would jump? What would you have done? Why? Use as many words as you can. Have fun, but make sense!

Word Wiggle ～～

Fill in the boxes around the word wiggle with the vocabulary word that best fits each clue. The first one has been done for you.

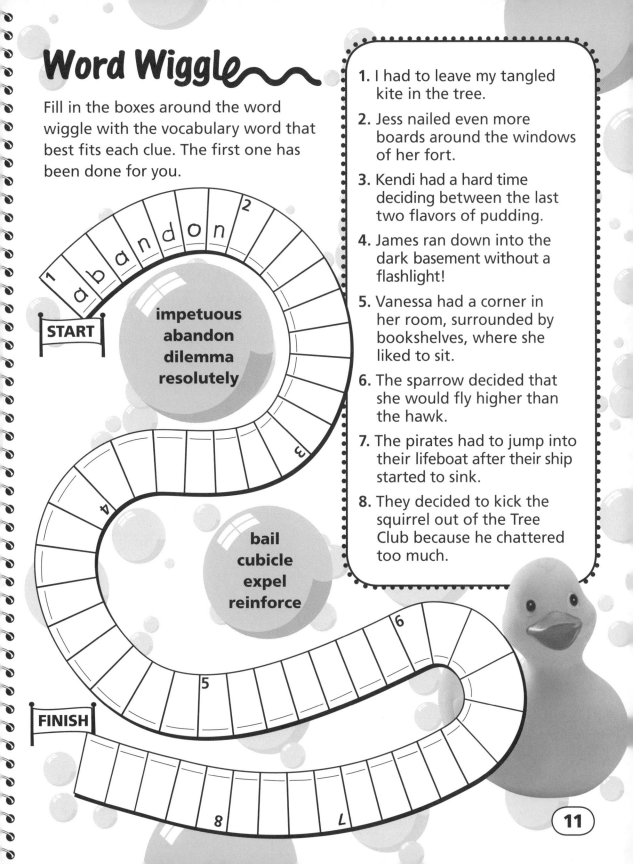

START

a b a n d o n

1 2

impetuous
abandon
dilemma
resolutely

3

4

bail
cubicle
expel
reinforce

5

6

FINISH

8 L

1. I had to leave my tangled kite in the tree.

2. Jess nailed even more boards around the windows of her fort.

3. Kendi had a hard time deciding between the last two flavors of pudding.

4. James ran down into the dark basement without a flashlight!

5. Vanessa had a corner in her room, surrounded by bookshelves, where she liked to sit.

6. The sparrow decided that she would fly higher than the hawk.

7. The pirates had to jump into their lifeboat after their ship started to sink.

8. They decided to kick the squirrel out of the Tree Club because he chattered too much.

11

In My Own Words

✔ Check the prompt that you want to write about. Then write a story using as many of the vocabulary words as possible. Have fun, but make sense!

☐ Think about a time when you did something without thinking about the danger it might put you in. What happened? Do you wish you had done things differently?

☐ Imagine that you're standing in front of two doors. Behind one door is a lot of money. Behind the other door is something you lost a long time ago. Which door would you choose if you could only open one door? Why? Was it difficult to choose?

☐ Think of your own story and write about it.

These are the words I used!

☐ cubicle   ☐ reinforce   ☐ abandon   ☐ dilemma

☐ bail   ☐ expel   ☐ impetuous   ☐ resolutely

TOTAL WORDS USED

Take It Further

| scoff | If you scoff at something, you talk about it in a way that shows you think it's silly. |

Benjamin's friends scoffed at him when

| assail | To assail something or someone is to attack them physically or verbally. |

Her sister's questions made Hilary feel like she was being assailed,

because

| optimistic | If you are optimistic, you are hopeful and look at things in a positive way. |

My sister is so optimistic about her singing ability that

| lament | If you lament something, you say how sad you are about it. |

The basketball team lamented to their coach after

| steadfast | If you are steadfast in doing something, you will not give up or be stopped from doing it. |

I remained steadfast during the long race by

| decisive | If you are decisive, you make decisions quickly without changing your mind later. |

Keisha is always decisive when it comes to

| gratifying | Something gratifying makes you feel happy and proud of what you've done. |

Ryan worked resolutely on his difficult math homework because

| resigned | If you are resigned to a bad situation, you accept it without complaining because you can't change it. |

Emilio finally became resigned to

15

- [ ] **scoff**
- [ ] **assail**
- [ ] **optimistic**
- [ ] **lament**
- [ ] **steadfast**
- [ ] **decisive**
- [ ] **gratifying**
- [ ] **resigned**

How Many Words Can I Use?

And still make sense!

Write about what you read in "What Do You Know?" What was your favorite part? Do you think the handwriting test really works? Use as many words as you can. Have fun, but make sense!

VOCABULARY JUMBLE

The vocabulary word that best fits each clue is hidden in the jumbled letters. Find the word and connect the letters. The first one has been done for you.

L	R	M	T
A	S	W	Y
M	E	N	T
O	A	D	H

P	L	S	O
S	R	C	T
M	A	O	F
K	U	Y	F

F	S	I	G
I	E	L	N
L	R	G	E
D	I	N	D

1. When I lost my mother's ring, I felt bad for three weeks.

2. I think that his idea is simply ridiculous.

3. He finally gave up on trying to learn how to sail.

D	E	K	E
I	N	S	V
D	E	X	I
C	C	I	S

T	P	O	J
I	E	N	A
M	I	S	C
A	U	T	I

4. I liked all the puppies, but I chose the brown one right away.

5. I am very sure that our team will win the contest!

decisive
steadfast
lament

scoff
optimistic
assail
gratifying
resigned

T	R	U	P
S	S	L	A
A	A	B	D
X	I	L	E

F	Y	I	N
I	A	U	G
T	A	R	G
E	L	S	Y

T	S	T	T
R	A	E	U
U	D	F	A
K	A	T	S

6. She pounded the door until it opened.

7. It felt so wonderful to receive the math award.

8. I will work hard every day until I have learned to skate.

In My Own Words

Check the prompt that you want to write about. Then write a story using as many of the vocabulary words as possible. Have fun, but make sense!

☐ Think about a time when you wanted to learn a new skill. What steps did you take to learn this skill? How did you feel when you finally reached your goal?

☐ Write a letter to a friend describing a time when you made a quick decision about something. Did it turn out the way you wanted? Did you wish that you had made another decision?

☐ Think of your own story and write about it.

TOTAL WORDS USED

✔ These are the words I used!

☐ scoff   ☐ optimistic   ☐ steadfast   ☐ gratifying
☐ assail   ☐ lament   ☐ decisive   ☐ resigned

Take It Further

eliminate	If you eliminate something, you remove it completely.

Akina eliminated one of her school activities because

stationary	Something that is stationary is not moving.

The squirrel heard a noise and remained stationary until

incredulous	If you are incredulous, you can't believe something because it is very surprising.

Mark became incredulous when

contender	A contender is someone who competes to win a contest or election, usually with a good chance of winning.

Anna was a strong contender for president because

grimace	When you grimace, you twist your face in an ugly way because you are in pain or don't like something.

Nikko grimaced when he

fatigue	If you feel fatigue, you feel very, very tired.

Brooke felt fatigued after

stamina	Someone who has stamina can do something tiring for a long time.

It was easy to see that I had a lot of stamina because

foil	If you foil someone's attempt to do something, you stop them from doing it.

Jamie foiled his new puppy's attempt to

- [ ] eliminate
- [ ] stationary
- [ ] incredulous
- [ ] contender
- [ ] grimace
- [ ] fatigue
- [ ] stamina
- [ ] foil

How Many Words Can I Use?

And still make sense!

Write about what you read in "Buried Treasure." How do you think Jill's grandfather will react when he sees the pumpkin? Will he take it to the contest? Write your own ending to the story. Use as many words as you can. Have fun, but make sense!

CROSSWORD PUZZLE

Word bank (top right): eliminate, incredulous, grimace, stamina

Word bank (left): stationary, contender, fatigue, foil

Down

1. Irina felt _____ set in, and she didn't think she could finish the race.
2. I am _____ whenever I hear stories about space monsters.
3. Paco had to _____ the other team's attempt to score.
4. Giana was a _____ in the pie-eating contest.

Across

5. I do not think I have the _____ to finish the hike.
6. I knew he was mad at me when I saw the _____ on his face.
7. The cement block did not move. It was completely _____.
8. The coach will have to _____ someone from the team.

In My Own Words

Check the prompt that you want to write about. Then write a story using as many of the vocabulary words as possible. Have fun, but make sense!

☐ Imagine that you are in a very strange contest. What is the contest for? Who else is in the contest? What is the prize?

☐ Think about a time when you were really embarrassed. Who or what embarrassed you? Why were you so embarrassed? Write a journal entry about it.

☐ Think of your own story and write about it.

Take It Further

fume	If you fume about something, you talk or think about it in an angry way.

Marcos started to fume when

rummage	Rummaging through something means searching for something you want by moving things around in a hurried way.

Please rummage through that drawer and

hypnotic	Something that is hypnotic holds your attention so much that you can't think of anything else.

Hypnotic is the only way to describe

opponent	An opponent is someone who is against you in a game, contest, or election.

I didn't see my opponent until

glum	If you are glum, you are sad and quiet because you are unhappy about something.

Ana felt glum when

dedication	If you show dedication to something, you give it a lot of time and effort because you care so much about it.

Akiko showed her dedication to music by

seclusion	If you are in seclusion, you are in a quiet place away from other people.

R.J. wanted to go into seclusion, so he

victorious	You are victorious if you win a contest, sport, or battle.

Because we were victorious, our team

How Many Words Can I Use?

And still make sense!

- [ ] **fume**
- [ ] **rummage**
- [ ] **hypnotic**
- [ ] **opponent**
- [ ] **glum**
- [ ] **dedication**
- [ ] **seclusion**
- [ ] **victorious**

Write about what you read in "Dragon Tales." What do you think happened in Scaly's next match? Did she win again? Use as many words as you can. Have fun, but make sense!

Word Riddles

Read the clues for each number. Then fill in the blanks with the correct vocabulary word. The first one has been done for you.

dedicated

fume

seclusion

rummage

glum

opponent

victorious

hypnotic

1. <u>glum</u>
- This is a sad word.
- It is an emotion.
- This word starts with a *g*.

2. _____
- This word has five vowels.
- This word is a reason to celebrate.
- You feel this way after you win a game.

3. _____
- This word is something you do.
- This word has seven letters.
- This word uses the letter *m* twice.

4. _____
- You would use this word when you were talking about a competition.
- This word describes a person.
- This word starts with a vowel.

5. _____
- This word has nine letters.
- To be this way, you have to work hard.
- This word uses the letter *d* three times.

6. _____
- This word is a way you feel.
- To feel this way, you have to be angry.
- This word has the same number of vowels and consonants.

7. _____
- This word has five consonants.
- This word is a place.
- If you are here, you might feel lonely.

8. _____
- This word has eight letters.
- Things like this are really, really interesting.
- This word starts with an *h*.

In My Own Words

Check the prompt that you want to write about. Then write a story using as many of the vocabulary words as possible. Have fun, but make sense!

☐ Think about a time when you really wanted to be good at something. What did you do to achieve your goal? What was the hardest part of reaching your goal? Write about it in a letter to your best friend.

☐ What is your favorite game? Why do you like it? Who do you play it with? What steps do you take when you play the game?

☐ Think of your own story and write about it.

TOTAL WORDS USED

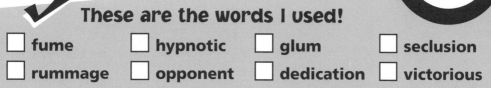

✓ These are the words I used!

- ☐ fume
- ☐ rummage
- ☐ hypnotic
- ☐ opponent
- ☐ glum
- ☐ dedication
- ☐ seclusion
- ☐ victorious

Take It Further

lodge	If an object lodges somewhere, it gets stuck there.

I knew the rock was lodged because

feverish	If you do something feverishly, you do it very quickly, as if you need to finish it as soon as possible

If he worked feverishly, Mike might

tactic	A tactic is something you do to try to get what you want.

When I started the race, my tactic was to

disband	If a group disbands, it stops doing things together as a group.

The team disbanded because

ingenuity	If you have ingenuity, you are good at finding new ways to solve problems and make things.

Julio showed ingenuity when

anonymous	If you are anonymous, other people don't know your name or that you were the one who did something.

The writer wanted to be anonymous because

crucial	If something is crucial, it is very important.

Practice is the most crucial part of playing the flute because

formative	A formative experience is one that plays an important part in the kind of person you become.

The actor's most formative experience was

- [ ] lodge
- [ ] feverish
- [ ] tactic
- [ ] disband
- [ ] ingenuity
- [ ] anonymous
- [ ] crucial
- [ ] formative

How Many Words Can I Use?

And still make sense!

Write about what you read in "Professor Detector and the Mysterious Moaner." Did you have any guesses about what might have been making the moaning sounds? What were they? What would the end of the story have been like if you had been right? Use as many words as you can. Have fun, but make sense!

VOCABULARY JUMBLE

The vocabulary word that best fits each clue is hidden in the jumbled letters. Find the word and connect the letters. The first one has been done for you.

1. No one knows who I am.

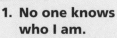

Z	A	N	O
O	M	Y	N
U	K	M	O
S	L	A	Y

2. I'm working hard and fast!

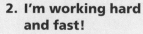

G	M	S	I
T	D	H	R
E	R	C	E
A	F	E	V

3. It's stuck!

L	A	D	T
N	N	E	U
O	D	G	E
L	Z	K	H

4. Break it up.

D	I	X	D
J	D	I	S
W	P	A	B
D	N	N	D

5. Super important!

S	A	L	C
C	H	Y	K
V	U	C	I
C	R	L	A

6. Good idea!

T	I	U	L
Y	L	N	I
N	G	E	R
I	T	Y	D

7. Here's the plan.

Y	Z	C	T
B	H	A	I
O	M	T	C
X	T	O	E

8. An important memory.

O	F	L	F
S	B	R	O
T	A	M	E
I	V	E	Y

In My Own Words

Check the prompt that you want to write about. Then write a story using as many of the vocabulary words as possible. Have fun, but make sense!

☐ What is the very first memory you have? Why is it important to you? Can you learn anything about yourself from it? Use that first memory to write a short autobiography of yourself when you were very young.

☐ Do you do chores at home? Write about what you do. Do you think the chores are hard or easy? What do you like most about them? What do you like least?

☐ Think of your own story and write about it.

Take It Further

| levitate | If someone or something levitates, they appear to rise and float in the air without anything to support them. |

The man in the movie levitated when

| neglect | If you neglect something, you fail to take care of it properly. |

Diana felt neglected because

| stifle | If you stifle something that is happening, you force it to stop. |

The umpire stifled the argument when

| astray | Something that has gone astray has gone missing while it is on its way somewhere. |

When I went astray, I

| alibi | If you have an alibi for something, you can prove that it was not your fault or you were somewhere else when it happened. |

After the crime, James told the police that his alibi was

| enigma | Something that is an enigma is mysterious and difficult to understand. |

Kara was an enigma to Cale because

| escapade | A daring adventure or action can be called an escapade. |

Cathy's last escapade happened when she

| notorious | To be notorious means to be well known for something bad. |

Some people are notorious for

- [ ] levitate
- [ ] neglect
- [ ] stifle
- [ ] astray
- [ ] alibi
- [ ] enigma
- [ ] escapade
- [ ] notorious

How Many Words Can I Use?

And still make sense!

Write about what you read in "Adventures on Lookout Lane." Do you think the friends that live on Lookout Lane have fun? Pretend you were invited to Lisa and Luis's birthday party. What was their party like? Who were their guests? What did everyone do? Use as many words as you can. Have fun, but make sense!

Word Wiggle

Fill in the boxes around the word wiggle with the vocabulary word that best fits each clue. The first one has been done for you.

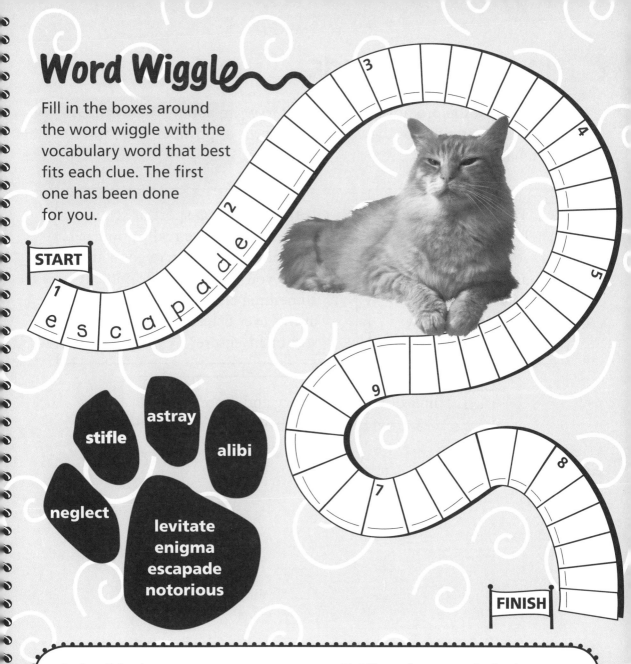

START

1. e s c a p a d e

2.

3.

4.

5.

9.

7.

8.

FINISH

stifle

astray

alibi

neglect

levitate
enigma
escapade
notorious

1. A wild adventure
2. The opposite of taking good care of something
3. Something a ghost might do
4. "I didn't do it! I was with Mom the whole time!"
5. Like a famous criminal
6. Hard to figure out
7. Stopping something from happening
8. Someone who wanders away

In My Own Words

Check the prompt that you want to write about. Then write a story using as many of the vocabulary words as possible. Have fun, but make sense!

☐ Think about the last time you did something exciting and unplanned with your friends. What did you do? How did you feel?

☐ Is there a certain sport or school subject that you're really good at? Do you like that you're good at it, or do you wish you were good at something else? Has being good at this ever helped you go on any sort of adventure?

☐ Think of your own story and write about it.

✔ **These are the words I used!**

- ☐ levitate
- ☐ neglect
- ☐ stifle
- ☐ astray
- ☐ alibi
- ☐ enigma
- ☐ escapade
- ☐ notorious

Take It Further

lurch	If you lurch, you make a sudden, jerky movement forward.

When the boat lurched, the passengers

primp	If you primp, you take a long time getting ready because you are picky about how you look.

My sister spends so much time primping that

putrid	Something that is putrid is rotten and smells awful.

Ronnie's old tennis shoes smell putrid because

rowdy	If people are rowdy, they are noisy and rough and may end up causing trouble.

The people at the concert were so rowdy that

| **jovial** | If someone is jovial, they are happy and behave in a cheerful way. |

Monica was jovial all day because

| **outlandish** | If something is outlandish, it is weird and unlikely to happen. |

Her hair looked outlandish because

| **allure** | The allure of something is the way it is attractive or exciting. |

The allure of diamonds is so strong that

| **suave** | Someone who is suave is charming, polite, and elegant but may not be sincere. |

That salesperson was so suave he

☑ **These are the words I used!**

- ☐ lurch
- ☐ primp
- ☐ putrid
- ☐ rowdy
- ☐ jovial
- ☐ outlandish
- ☐ allure
- ☐ suave

How Many Words Can I Use?

And still make sense!

Write about what you read in "Discovering Dolphins." Did you find out anything new about dolphins? Do you know something about dolphins that wasn't in the magazine? What do you think your life would be like if you had a dolphin friend? Use as many words as you can. Have fun, but make sense!

Hidden Clues

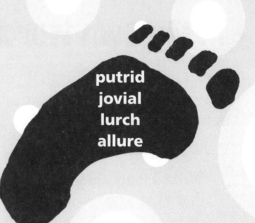

putrid
jovial
lurch
allure

Fill in the blanks with the vocabulary word that best fits each clue. The letters in the boxes will spell out the answer to the question at the bottom of the page. The first one has been done for you.

1. What a sudden start! l u r c [1 h]

2. That is so unlikely! __ __ __ __ [2 __] __ __ __ __

3. How does my hair look? [3 __] __ __ __ [4 __]

4. Ew! What stinks? __ __ __ __ [5 __] __

suave
rowdy
outlandish
primp

5. Settle down! __ __ __ __ [6 __]

6. I'm so happy! __ __ [7 __] __ __ __

7. He always tells me how nice I look. __ __ [8 __] __ [9 __]

8. I really want to go there! It looks so interesting.

__ __ __ __ [10 __] __

How did Rrrrrella and the Prince live?

__ __ __ __ __ l __ e __ e r __ f t __ __
1   2   3   4   5   6   7   8   9   10

In My Own Words

Check the prompt that you want to write about. Then write a story using as many of the vocabulary words as possible. Have fun, but make sense!

☐ Write a magazine article that talks about something that smells really bad. What is it? Who found it?

☐ Would you want to win a contest and collect the prize? What contest would it be? What would you hope to win?

☐ Think of your own story and write about it.

TOTAL WORDS USED

✓ **These are the words I used!**

- ☐ lurch
- ☐ primp
- ☐ putrid
- ☐ rowdy
- ☐ jovial
- ☐ outlandish
- ☐ allure
- ☐ suave

49

Take It Further

jolt	If something gives you a jolt, it moves you in a sudden and hard way.

I could tell that someone had jolted Adam because

pry	If you pry something that is stuck, you force it to move or open.

Michelle and Yolanda had to pry the door by

prospect	The prospect of something is the chance that it might happen.

The prospect of Andre becoming a movie star is good because

incident	An incident is an event, usually an unpleasant one.

Sean said that the incident happened when

| **dumbfounded** | When you are dumbfounded, you are so surprised that you don't know what to say. |

Roberto was dumbfounded when

| **vindicate** | A person who is vindicated is proved to be right after others said they were wrong. |

Kyle had always said his restaurant was the best, so he felt vindicated when

| **isolated** | If something is isolated, it is separate and away from everything else. |

Looking at Anna's pictures, I knew her home was isolated because

| **refurbish** | If you refurbish something, you make it look like it did when it was new. |

Hannah wanted to refurbish her grandmother's chairs because

- [ ] **jolt**
- [ ] **pry**
- [ ] **prospect**
- [ ] **incident**
- [ ] **dumbfounded**
- [ ] **vindicate**
- [ ] **isolated**
- [ ] **refurbish**

How Many Words Can I Use?

And still make sense!

Write about what you read in "Kid Ninjas." How long do you think you have to train to be a real ninja? Which of the ninja skills was most impressive to you? Use as many words as you can. Have fun, but make sense!

VOCABULARY JUMBLE

The vocabulary word that best fits each clue is hidden in the jumbled letters. Find the word and connect the letters. The first one has been done for you.

jolt
pry
vindicated
isolated
refurbish
dumbfounded
prospects
incident

1. I'm going to have to _____ this old piano to make it look like it used to.

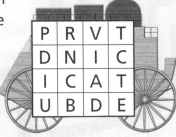

2. I felt _____ when everyone realized they had been wrong.

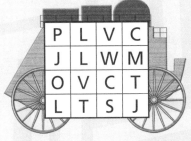

3. We'll have to _____ the lid off this can; it's stuck!

4. The static electricity gave Heather quite a _____.

5. I wish our _____ of winning were better.

6. That tree is _____ in the middle of the desert.

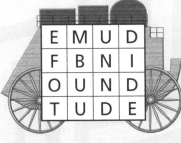

7. I was _____ when I realized I had ten hours of homework.

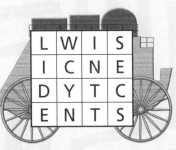

8. My dog ate my homework—it was quite an unfortunate _____.

In My Own Words

Check the prompt that you want to write about. Then write a story using as many of the vocabulary words as possible. Have fun, but make sense!

☐ Think about a time when you explored a new place, like a basement or a park. What did it look like? Did you discover anything? What happened while you were there?

☐ Write a journal entry about a time when something got broken. How did it break? Did it get fixed? How did you feel when it broke?

☐ Think of your own story and write about it.

These are the words I used!

☐ jolt   ☐ prospect   ☐ dumbfounded   ☐ isolated

☐ pry   ☐ incident   ☐ vindicate   ☐ refurbish

TOTAL WORDS USED

Take It Further

navigate	If you navigate something, you find a way to move on, through, or around it.

To navigate through the desert, we will need

phenomenal	Someone or something that is phenomenal is unusual because it is so good.

Ronnie knew he could be a phenomenal artist if he just

sedate	If a person or animal is sedate, they are quiet and don't get excited easily.

Jessica's cat was so sedate that

mandate	If you mandate something, you declare it must be done.

The king mandated that

astute	Someone who is astute is very good at understanding things.

We knew Sandra was astute when she

superior	If something is superior, it is far better than something else.

The book was superior to the movie because

humanitarian	A humanitarian works to improve the lives of people who are suffering.

Claude showed he was a humanitarian when he

accolade	If someone is given an accolade, something is done or said about them that shows how much people admire them.

Trina deserved the accolade because she had worked hard to

These are the words I used!

These are the words I used!

- [ ] navigate
- [ ] phenomenal
- [ ] sedate
- [ ] mandate
- [ ] astute
- [ ] superior
- [ ] humanitarian
- [ ] accolade

How Many Words Can I Use?

And still make sense!

Write about what you read in "Busting the Boot Squad." What do you think would happen if Baron Von Bootstrap came back? Would Christine defeat him? Use as many words as you can. Have fun, but make sense!

CROSS WORD PUZZLE

sedate
phenomenal
accolade
mandate

astute
humanitarian
navigate
superior

Across
1. If you keep talking so loudly, Mr. Green will _____ that we can't talk during lunch.
2. Ben's bike was _____ to Samuel's because it could go faster.
3. Randy should receive an _____ for all his hard work.
4. Tutoring kids after school proved Brynn was a _____.

Down
5. Timmy was so _____, that we never had to rock him to sleep.
6. The goalie's performance was _____. It was great!
7. We didn't know Janelle was so _____ until she got an A on the test.
8. The map really helped us _____ through the lake.

In My Own Words

Check the prompt that you want to write about. Then write a story using as many of the vocabulary words as possible. Have fun, but make sense!

☐ Think about a time when you did something nice for somebody or a group of people. What did you do? How did you feel afterward? Did you receive any awards for what you did?

☐ Write about a fictional character. Maybe they have a special power or maybe they're just really good at something. Write a biography of their life.

☐ Think of your own story and write about it.

These are the words I used!

TOTAL WORDS USED

- [ ] navigate
- [ ] phenomenal
- [ ] sedate
- [ ] mandate
- [ ] astute
- [ ] superior
- [ ] humanitarian
- [ ] accolade

Take It Further

thrive	When someone thrives, they do well and are successful, healthy, or strong.

Derrick thrives on attention because

aroma	Something's aroma is how it smells.

Roger woke up to the aroma of

coordination	A person with good coordination can move several parts of their body at the same time without getting mixed up.

My cousin is so coordinated that she can

surly	Someone who is surly behaves in a rude, bad-tempered way.

When Louisa gets up in the morning she is surly, and we all

know it because

pulverize	When you pulverize something, you crush, pound, or grind it into tiny pieces.

When the huge rocks were pulverized, they looked like

adversary	If you are competing against or fighting with someone, they are your adversary.

Stephanie and Pat have always been adversaries because

antic	Antics are funny, silly, or unusual ways of acting.

Jose knew the monkey in the zoo was up to his usual antics because

he was

mortify	If something mortifies you, it offends or embarrasses you a great deal.

When I got to school, I was mortified to find out that

☐ thrive
☐ aroma
☐ coordination
☐ surly
☐ pulverize
☐ adversary
☐ antic
☐ mortify

How Many Words Can I Use?

And still make sense!

Write about what you read in "A President's Best Friend." Do you like dogs? If you could have any kind of pet in the world, what would it be? What would the two of you do together? Use as many words as you can. Have fun, but make sense!

Hidden Clues

Fill in the blanks with the vocabulary word that best fits each clue. The letters in the boxes will spell out the answer to the question at the bottom of the page. The first one has been done for you.

thrive
aroma
coordination
surly
pulverize
adversary
antics
mortify

1. It's a way to describe the smell of rain.

a r [o] m a

2. That plant is doing really well!

__ __ __ __ __ __

3. Paul is jumping up and down, making crazy noises!

__ __ [2] __ __ __ __

4. I can rub my stomach and pat my head at the same time!

__ [3] __ __ __ __ __ __ __ __ __ __

5. I can't stand her. She's always trying to beat me at everything!

__ __ __ __ __ [4] __ __ __

6. You don't have to act that way, just because I won and you lost!

__ __ __ [5] __ __

7. John's joke was so gross, we all blushed. __ __ __ __ __ __ __

8. How did that big rock get into so many pieces?

__ __ __ __ __ [6] __ __ __ [7] __ __

What is the only thing Hank can do without being yelled at?

G __ __ __ __ __ __ __ p
   1   2   3   4   5   6   7

In My Own Words

Check the prompt that you want to write about. Then write a story using as many of the vocabulary words as possible. Have fun, but make sense!

☐ Write a poem about someone who is blamed for something that isn't their fault. How do they feel? What do they do? How do the people around them act?

☐ What is your favorite food? Your favorite smell? Favorite sport? Favorite subject? Why? How long have they been your favorite things? Do you think they'll be your favorites forever?

☐ Think of your own story and write about it.

Take It Further

ricochet	When something ricochets, it hits a surface and bounces back from it.

The rock ricocheted off the table and

fragment	A fragment of something is a small piece or part of it.

The fragment Morgan found was

radiance	Something's radiance is a glowing light that shines from it.

The radiance of the candle made Dion

dwindle	If something dwindles, it becomes smaller, weaker, or fewer in number.

While we were camping, we knew our food supply was dwindling when

auspicious	Something that is auspicious is a sign that more good things are on the way.

Winning the game was an auspicious moment for Brian because
after that

fleeting	If something is fleeting, it only lasts for a short time.

The group was sad, but only for a fleeting moment, because

fathom	If you cannot fathom something, you can't understand it, no matter how much you think about it.

Nicola could not fathom how

newsworthy	Something that is newsworthy is interesting enough to be reported in newspapers, on the radio, or on television.

What made Rosy's story newsworthy was the fact that

These are the words I used!

☑

- ☐ ricochet
- ☐ fragment
- ☐ radiance
- ☐ dwindle
- ☐ auspicious
- ☐ fleeting
- ☐ fathom
- ☐ newsworthy

How Many Words Can I Use?

And still make sense!

Write about what you read in "Food Fright." Write about the next adventure the food in the fridge has. Use as many words as you can. Have fun, but make sense!

Word Riddles

Read the clues for each number. Then fill in the blanks with the correct vocabulary word. The first one has been done for you.

newsworthy
ricochet
fathom

auspicious
dwindle

fragment
fleeting
radiance

1. <u>fleeting</u>
   - This is something that comes and goes quickly.
   - This word has three vowels.
   - This word rhymes with *cheating.*

2. _____
   - This is an action word.
   - A tennis ball does this.
   - The letter *c* is used twice in this word.

3. _____
   - This word has two syllables.
   - Glass breaks into these.
   - This word starts with an *f.*

4. _____
   - This word describes finding a four-leaf clover.
   - This word has six vowels.
   - This word rhymes with *delicious.*

5. _____
   - This is a description word.
   - You could use this word about a bank robbery.
   - This word is made up of two smaller words.

6. _____
   - This word means you have to think.
   - You would try to do this with a complicated problem.
   - This word has six letters.

7. _____
   - The sun has this.
   - You wouldn't use this word if you were talking about a thundercloud.
   - The letter *a* is in this word twice.

8. _____
   - This word describes something that keeps shrinking.
   - Daylight does this at sunset.
   - The letter *d* is in this word twice.

In My Own Words

Check the prompt that you want to write about. Then write a story using as many of the vocabulary words as possible. Have fun, but make sense!

☐ Think about something unusual you have seen recently. What happened? When and where did it happen? Who was involved? Write a newspaper article about what happened.

☐ Have you ever gazed at the stars? Where did you go? What did you see? Did you use a telescope, or just look up at the night sky?

☐ Think of your own story and write about it.

Take It Further

muster	If you muster something, you gather as much of it as you can in order to do something.

David mustered all his friends for

compact	If you compact something, you press it together to make it smaller or more solid.

We compacted the boxes so we could

scrawl	If you scrawl something, you write it in a careless and messy way.

Chandra scrawled a note to her mother about

crevice	A narrow crack or gap is called a crevice.

We looked into the crevice and saw

seldom	If something seldom happens, it only happens every once in a while.

I seldom ride the bus because

repulsive	Something that is repulsive is so horrible and disgusting that you want to avoid it.

Jason thinks spiders are repulsive because they

tolerate	If you tolerate something, you accept it even though you don't like it.

Every night, the neighbors have to tolerate Josiah's

teem	If a place is teeming with people or animals, it is crowded and the people or animals are moving around a lot.

When he saw that the room was teeming with ants, he

How Many Words Can I Use?

And still make sense!

Write about what you read in "Sand Notes." What if Sadie hadn't caught up to Avery on the beach that day? What do you think their next messages to each other would have been? What do you think would have happened if they hadn't met until the end of the summer? Use as many words as you can. Have fun, but make sense!

VOCABULARY JUMBLE

The vocabulary word that best fits each clue is hidden in the jumbled letters. Find the word and connect the letters. The first one has been done for you.

X	L	U	W
I	S	P	O
V	T	E	F
E	M	R	Z

1. That's disgusting!

D	U	M	C
R	W	U	S
G	N	Y	T
J	D	R	E

2. I'm trying to get my strength together.

C	R	E	V
P	E	C	I
Y	T	R	Q
H	Z	O	H

3. Crack.

compact
scrawl
seldom
muster
teeming
repulsive
crevice
tolerate

H	C	E	L
B	K	D	S
Y	M	U	E
A	O	D	L

4. Hardly ever.

L	C	S	A
T	R	K	H
E	V	N	G
E	M	I	L

5. It's so crowded!

T	C	O	M
S	O	L	P
D	C	U	A
R	U	T	C

6. Squash.

L	E	R	T
B	Y	A	O
A	R	E	L
T	E	B	P

7. I have to deal with it.

G	S	C	L
W	O	R	J
E	D	A	W
A	N	R	L

8. Scribble.

In My Own Words

Check the prompt that you want to write about. Then write a story using as many of the vocabulary words as possible. Have fun, but make sense!

☐ Write a journal entry about the most awful place you've ever been. What was so bad about it? Why didn't you like it? How would you change it?

☐ Pretend that you and your best friend are on a camping trip in the mountains. What do you do? Where do you go? What kind of adventures do you have?

☐ Think of your own story and write about it.

These are the words I used!

- ☑
- ☐ muster
- ☐ compact
- ☐ scrawl
- ☐ crevice
- ☐ seldom
- ☐ repulsive
- ☐ tolerate
- ☐ teem

TOTAL WORDS USED

79

Take It Further

dainty	Something that is dainty is delicate, small, and pretty.

Laura thought the doll looked dainty because it

eloquent	If you are eloquent, you use words well to say what you mean and get people to think like you.

His eloquent note made me

shard	A sharp and pointy piece of broken glass, pottery, or metal is called a shard.

Those shards of glass are on the floor because

torment	If something torments you, it causes you great mental or physical suffering.

The children were tormented by

disheveled	If someone looks disheveled, their hair or clothes are very messy.

Robbie looks disheveled because he

excruciating	Something that is excruciating is very, very painful.

Looking at his report card was excruciating for Robin because

fickle	If someone is fickle, they change their mind a lot about what they think or want.

Katie is fickle, especially when

overreact	If you overreact to a situation, you respond to it more strongly than you should.

My father said I overreacted when

- ☐ **dainty**
- ☐ **eloquent**
- ☐ **shard**
- ☐ **torment**
- ☐ **disheveled**
- ☐ **excruciating**
- ☐ **fickle**
- ☐ **overreact**

How Many Words Can I Use?

And still make sense!

Write about what you read in "Dream Ship." What if you were the person going around the world in Captain Nick's ship? Where would you go? What would you see? Use as many words as you can. Have fun, but make sense!

Word Wiggle

Fill in the boxes around the word wiggle with the vocabulary word that best fits each clue. The first one has been done for you.

excruciating
fickle
eloquent
torment
overreact
dainty
disheveled
shard

START

1. f i c k l e

2.

3.

4.

5.

6.

7.

8.

1. You always change your mind!
2. You speak so well!
3. These pieces of glass are sharp, watch out.

4. Calm down; it's not that bad!
5. He's a mess!
6. Quit bothering me!
7. It's so tiny and pretty!
8. Oh, the pain!

FINISH

In My Own Words

Check the prompt that you want to write about. Then write a story using as many of the vocabulary words as possible. Have fun, but make sense!

☐ Write a fairy tale. You can include any characters you want: princesses and princes, dragons, monsters, elves—it's up to you! Think of a problem for your characters to solve.

☐ Do you have a pet? What if your pet cat started talking to you one day? What do you think she would say? What would the two of you do together?

☐ Think of your own story and write about it.

These are the words I used!

☐ dainty   ☐ shard   ☐ disheveled   ☐ fickle

☐ eloquent   ☐ torment   ☐ excruciating   ☐ overreact

TOTAL WORDS USED

Take It Further

epidemic	If there is an epidemic of something, it affects a large number of people and spreads quickly.

A chicken pox epidemic would

detach	If you detach something, you remove or separate it from another thing.

The instructions said to detach the

evidently	If something is evidently true, there is proof that it is true.

Luke and Ryan were evidently friends, because they

gaze	Someone's gaze is how they are looking at something, especially when they are looking steadily at it.

When the teacher called on Felipe today, he was gazing

destiny	If something is your destiny, it will happen to you and you cannot change it.

It was Tony's destiny to

bleak	If a situation is bleak, it is bad and unlikely to get better.

Monday was really bleak, mostly because

presume	If you presume that something is so, you think it is so, but you are not sure.

She presumed Leon wasn't guilty, but

rebuff	If you rebuff someone, you rudely refuse them and make them go away.

Shannon's rebuff hurt Paul because

How Many Words Can I Use?

And still make sense!

Write about what you read in "The Dog-Cat Rap."
What was your favorite part of the rap? What did
you agree with? What did you disagree with? Use as
many words as you can. Have fun, but make sense!

Word Riddles

Read the clues for each number. Then fill in the blanks with the correct vocabulary word. The first one has been done for you.

Word list (thermometer):
detach
gaze
presume
evidently
bleak
rebuff
epidemic
destiny

1. _destiny_
- You can't change this.
- A synonym for this word is fate.
- This word starts with a *d*.

2. _____
- This is an action word.
- You might do this if you saw something very beautiful.
- This word has four letters.

3. _____
- He thought she was innocent but wasn't sure.
- You might know this, but you might not.
- There are three vowels in this word.

4. _____
- There's been an outbreak of the flu in our town.
- This could send you to the doctor!
- This word starts with an *e*.

5. _____
- This is how you take something apart.
- Pen caps do this.
- This word starts with *d*.

6. _____
- When you think something is true, you can use this word.
- This word ends in a *y*.
- This word has three vowels.

7. _____
- This word describes days that are just not good.
- Five of the nine players were hurt, they probably weren't going to win this game.
- This word has five letters.

8. _____
- Your feelings would be hurt if someone did this to you.
- This word ends in two consonants.
- This word is six letters long.

In My Own Words

✔ Check the prompt that you want to write about. Then write a story using as many of the vocabulary words as possible. Have fun, but make sense!

☐ Have your parents ever gotten upset with you for something that wasn't your fault? What was it? Did you explain to them that you didn't do it? Did they listen to you?

☐ Do you feel like you have to do a certain thing? What is it? Why? Are you excited about it? Write a journal entry explaining all of this.

☐ Think of your own story and write about it.

Take It Further

possession	Your possessions are the things you own.

The book is Jonathan's favorite possession because

venture	If you venture somewhere, you go somewhere even though it might be dangerous.

They decided to take a risk and ventured into

scarcely	You use scarcely to say that something is just barely the case.

Isn't that test going to be hard since you scarcely

keen	If someone is keen, they are very aware and able to see even the most minor details.

Logan is so keen that he

scrutinize	When you scrutinize something, you look at it very closely and carefully.

Madison scrutinized the snow globe, amazed that

quandary	If you are in a quandary, you have to make a decision but can't decide what to do.

Meg was in a quandary when she had to

elucidate	If you elucidate something, you make it clear and easy to understand.

After Mr. Garza handed out the homework assignment, he

elucidated on

plentiful	If something is plentiful, there is so much of it that there's enough for everyone.

The strawberries in the field were plentiful, so we

How Many Words Can I Use?

And still make sense!

☐ possession
☐ venture
☐ scarcely
☐ keen
☐ scrutinize
☐ quandary
☐ elucidate
☐ plentiful

Write about what you read in "Nighttime Noises." What was your favorite thing? Which part did you think was the most interesting? Did you think anything was funny? What other nighttime noises do you hear? Use as many words as you can. Have fun, but make sense!

Hidden Clues

Fill in the blanks with the vocabulary word that best fits each clue. The letters in the boxes will spell out the answer to the question at the bottom of the page. The first one has been done for you.

1. Before you turn in your test, _____ it, so there aren't any mistakes.

   s c r u [t] i n i z [e]

2. I can't decide which team to play on. I'm in a _____.

   __ __ __ __ __ __ __ __ [3]

3. You must be very _____ to notice such a tiny bug. __ [4] __ __

4. You're almost late. You _____ made it on time!

   __ [5] [6] __ __ __ __ __

5. I don't get it. Please _____.

   __ __ __ [7] __ __ __ __ __

6. Mom gave me that ring, so it's my _____, not yours.

   __ __ __ __ __ __ __ __ [8] [9] __ __

7. Fred loves to be outside. He always _____ out—no matter how awful the weather is.

   [10] __ __ __ __ __ __

8. Everybody come have some! The watermelon is _____ today!

   [11] __ __ __ __ __ __ __

**possession
scarcely
scrutinize
elucidate
ventures
keen
quandary
plentiful**

What happened to the four smart men?

__ h __ __ b __ __ __ me __ __ u __ s __ __ o r s.
1   2 3   4 5 6   7 8   9   10 11

In My Own Words

Check the prompt that you want to write about. Then write a story using as many of the vocabulary words as possible. Have fun, but make sense!

☐ Imagine living in a place where it is night all the time. What would your life be like without the sun? What would be different?

☐ Have you ever predicted something? What did you predict? Were you right?

☐ Think of your own story and write about it.

Take It Further

skim	If something skims over something else, it moves very quickly along the top of it.

The bird skimmed over the water by

insistent	If you say something in an insistent way, you keep telling people that it is so, even if they disagree.

Charlotte was very insistent about

unscathed	If you are unscathed after something dangerous happens, you have not been hurt by it.

They were lucky to escape unscathed because

subtle	If something is subtle, you may not notice it right away because it doesn't stand out.

The sound was subtle, but Erica

maneuver	When you maneuver something, you move it for a particular reason.

Andrew tried to maneuver the shopping cart around

intense	When something is intense, it is very strong or goes to an extreme degree.

The sun was so intense that

audacious	An audacious person tries some wild things, even taking risks, to reach their goals.

We could not believe how audacious Madeline was when

fanatical	Someone is fanatical if they feel so strongly about something that it's almost crazy.

Mrs. Fountain, my math teacher, is fanatical about

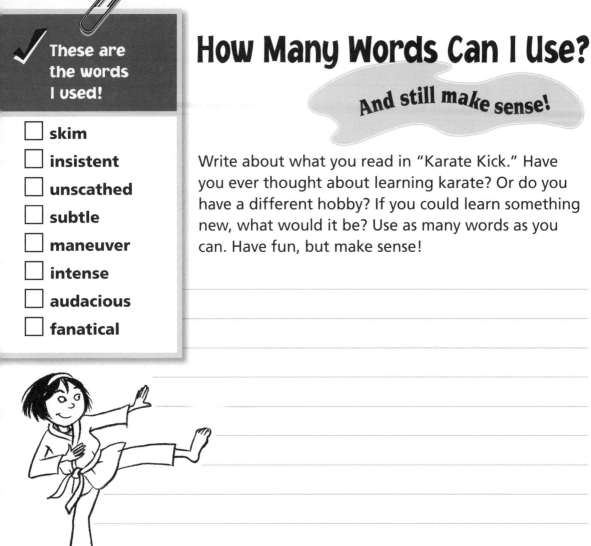

These are the words I used!

- [ ] skim
- [ ] insistent
- [ ] unscathed
- [ ] subtle
- [ ] maneuver
- [ ] intense
- [ ] audacious
- [ ] fanatical

How Many Words Can I Use?

And still make sense!

Write about what you read in "Karate Kick." Have you ever thought about learning karate? Or do you have a different hobby? If you could learn something new, what would it be? Use as many words as you can. Have fun, but make sense!

Word Riddles

subtle   maneuver
unscathed   insistent
intense   audacious
fanatical   skim

Read the clues for each number. Then fill in the blanks with the correct vocabulary word. The first one has been done for you.

1. <u>skim</u>
   - In order to do this, you have to be over the top of something.
   - This word has three consonants.
   - Some people do this with stones over water.

2. _____
   - This word has four vowels.
   - This is a movement word.
   - This word starts with an *m*.

3. _____
   - You're very daring!
   - This word starts with a vowel.
   - Someone who does wild things could be described this way.

4. _____
   - There wasn't a scratch on him!
   - After an accident, you're lucky if you're this word.
   - This word has nine letters.

5. _____
   - This word starts with a consonant.
   - A person who is this way feels strongly about something.
   - This word rhymes with *radical*.

6. _____
   - This type of person might argue with you.
   - This person just keeps telling people the same thing.
   - The letter *s* is in this word twice.

7. _____
   - This word describes something that doesn't stand out.
   - This word starts with an *s*.
   - Quiet and not flashy.

8. _____
   - This word has seven letters.
   - Something powerful could be described this way.
   - Very strong.

In My Own Words

✔ Check the prompt that you want to write about. Then write a story using as many of the vocabulary words as possible. Have fun, but make sense!

☐ Write an article about a sports game. It can be a real sport or one you just made up, but make sure to tell all about the action and what happened. Who won?

☐ What was your most exciting day ever? What happened? Would you go back and change anything if you could?

☐ Think of your own story and write about it.

These are the words I used!

- [ ] skim
- [ ] insistent
- [ ] unscathed
- [ ] subtle
- [ ] maneuver
- [ ] intense
- [ ] audacious
- [ ] fanatical

TOTAL WORDS USED

Take It Further

| prosper | If someone prospers, they are successful and do very well. |

Ana knew she would prosper because she

| reputation | Your reputation is what you are known for or what other people think of you. |

I don't know why that store has such a good reputation,

because

| transpire | When something transpires a certain way, it happens or develops that way. |

All of these events—losing the dog, breaking my arm, and forgetting

my homework—transpired after

| squander | If you squander money or a chance to do something, you waste it for a foolish reason. |

Josh squandered his money on

flabbergasted	Someone who is flabbergasted is so surprised that they don't know what to think.

Allen was flabbergasted when he found out

altercation	An altercation is a noisy argument or disagreement.

It is always smart to avoid an altercation because

speculate	If you speculate about something, you make guesses about what it is or what might happen.

Even though the game didn't start for twenty minutes, Hope was already speculating that

verify	If you verify something, you carefully check to make sure that it is true.

Ms. Jones decided to verify Caroline's excuse by

How Many Words Can I Use?

And still make sense!

- [ ] prosper
- [ ] reputation
- [ ] transpire
- [ ] squander
- [ ] flabbergasted
- [ ] altercation
- [ ] speculate
- [ ] verify

Write about what you read in "Bloomer Blog." What do you think life was like for a Bloomer Girl? How do you think your life is different from theirs? Use as many words as you can. Have fun, but make sense!

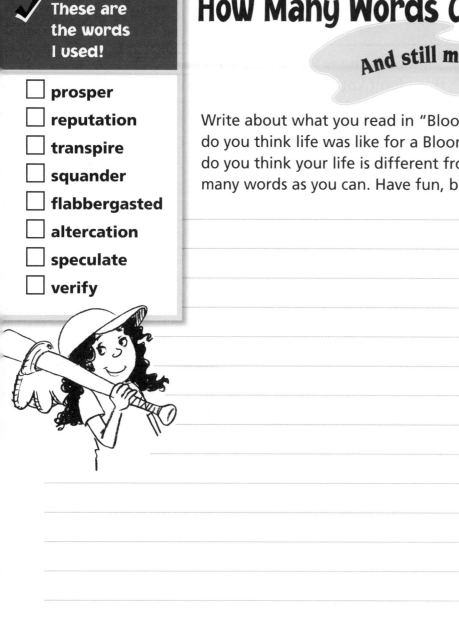

CROSSWORD PUZZLE

transpire
flabbergasted
speculate
squander

prosper
reputation
verify
altercation

Across
1. what people think of you
2. surprised
3. happen
4. check

Down
5. guess
6. throw away
7. fight
8. succeed

107

In My Own Words

Check the prompt that you want to write about. Then write a story using as many of the vocabulary words as possible. Have fun, but make sense!

☐ Pretend that you've just broken a world record. Write a letter to a friend telling them what the record was, how you broke it, and why you're excited.

☐ When was the last time you had a fight with someone? Who was it? What was the fight about? Was one of you right in the end?

☐ Think of your own story and write about it.

TOTAL WORDS USED

✔ **These are the words I used!**

☐ prosper ☐ transpire ☐ flabbergasted ☐ speculate

☐ reputation ☐ squander ☐ altercation ☐ verify

Take It Further

texture	The texture of something is the way it feels when you touch it.

Ferdinand said the texture of the wall was

consistent	Things that are consistent act, happen, or look about the same each time.

Anna went to bed at a consistent time every night so

jaunt	A jaunt is a short trip that you go on for fun.

Micah and Xavier went on a jaunt to

extravaganza	If something is an extravaganza, it is extremely fantastic and amazing.

The class party became an extravaganza when

expedition	If you go on an expedition, you take an important trip to reach a particular goal.

Adam loved camping, but this expedition was special

because

amiable	If you are amiable, you are friendly and people like being around you.

Tuan showed how amiable he is when

indomitable	Someone who is indomitable never gives up or admits defeat.

Elizabeth is so indomitable that in the race last week she

vivacious	If you are vivacious, you are lively and exciting.

The vivacious girls were all

How Many Words Can I Use?

And still make sense!

- [ ] texture
- [ ] consistent
- [ ] jaunt
- [ ] extravaganza
- [ ] expedition
- [ ] amiable
- [ ] indomitable
- [ ] vivacious

Write about what you read in "Find it in the Future." What else do you think people will use in the future? How do you think those things will be advertised? Use as many words as you can. Have fun, but make sense!

Hidden Clues

Fill in the blanks with the vocabulary word that best fits each clue. The letters in the boxes will spell out the answer to the question at the bottom of the page. The first one has been done for you.

1. She never quits!   i n d o m i t a [b] l e

2. Jane is so full of life!   _ _ _ _ _ _ [2] _ _

3. This cookie dough is soft and gooey.   _ _ _ _ _ [3] _

4. We went on a quick trip to the park.   _ _ _ [4]

5. Doug and Sally went to Africa to study wild animals.

   _ _ _ _ _ _ [5] _ _ _

6. The athletic banquet was the biggest, fanciest event I've ever attended.

   _ _ _ [6] [7] [8] _ _ _ _ _ _

7. Frank is always happy to do things for other people.

   _ _ _ _ _ _ _

8. I do really well in this part of the game every time.

   _ _ _ _ _ _ [9] _ _

What was Owney born to do?

He was _ _ _ _ to
     1 2 3 4

_ _ _ _ _ l.
5 6 7 8 9

amiable
extravaganza
consistent
texture
jaunt
expedition
vivacious
indomitable

In My Own Words

Check the prompt that you want to write about. Then write a story using as many of the vocabulary words as possible. Have fun, but make sense!

☐ Write a biography of a great explorer you know about, or one you wish existed. Write about their life and tell about their adventures. Did they have fun?

☐ If you could go on vacation anywhere in the world, where would you go? Who would you go with? What would you do?

☐ Think of your own story and write about it.

These are the words I used!

- [ ] texture
- [ ] consistent
- [ ] jaunt
- [ ] extravaganza
- [ ] expedition
- [ ] amiable
- [ ] indomitable
- [ ] vivacious

Take It Further

| mischief | Mischief is something that irritates or annoys people but doesn't seriously hurt anyone or anything. |

Marilise got into some mischief when she

| recruit | If you recruit people for something you are doing, you convince them to help you do it. |

Matt had to recruit his friends for

| nonchalant | If someone is nonchalant, they seem calm and don't seem to worry about what happens. |

Won was nonchalant about losing this contest because

| undeterred | If you are undeterred, you keep doing something, even when other people try to stop you. |

While building her castle, Queen Georgina was undeterred, even

when

meander	Someone or something that meanders somewhere moves slowly and not in a straight line.

Mom knew we had meandered home because

apprehension	If you feel apprehension, you are afraid that something bad might happen.

Tina felt apprehensive when she saw

sleuth	A sleuth is someone who solves mysteries or investigates crimes.

Jennifer knew she was a good sleuth when

hunch	If you have a hunch about something, you have a strong feeling it is true, even though you don't have any proof.

I had a hunch my brothers were throwing me a surprise party

because

How Many Words Can I Use?

And still make sense!

Write about what you read in "Weird Laws." What did you think of the laws? Write a newspaper article about someone breaking one of the weird laws you read about. Use as many words as you can. Have fun, but make sense!

VOCABULARY JUMBLE

The vocabulary word that best fits each clue is hidden in the jumbled letters. Find the word and connect the letters. The first one has been done for you.

recruit
nonchalant
mischief
apprehension
undeterred
hunch
meandering
sleuth

F	A	P	R
A	P	H	E
L	T	F	C
Y	T	U	R

1. Dan wants to _____ some friends for a snowball fight.

F	E	H	E
P	R	W	N
P	C	U	S
A	N	O	I

2. I feel some _____ when I see a spider.

N	O	N	C
A	L	A	H
N	T	U	P
C	N	P	R

3. Kayla tried to act _____, so no one would suspect her.

S	M	E	N
L	I	T	T
E	S	C	H
H	F	E	I

4. Mom's going to yell if you keep getting into _____!

A	M	O	C
P	A	N	D
R	E	M	E
G	N	I	R

5. "You're always _____ —it takes you forever to get anywhere!"

S	L	C	S
X	H	N	I
H	C	R	T
D	N	U	H

6. I have a _____ that Roger is taking my cookies.

R	E	P	P
R	T	E	A
E	C	D	N
D	T	H	U

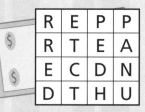

7. He might be seven points ahead, but I'm _____.

R	U	T	H
D	E	G	R
S	L	D	C
U	N	M	I

8. "You figured out where the jewelry was. You're a _____!"

In My Own Words

✓ Check the prompt that you want to write about. Then write a story using as many of the vocabulary words as possible. Have fun, but make sense!

☐ Write a poem about the detectives at a detective agency called *We can Solve It*. Are the detectives good at their job? What kind of crimes do they solve? How do they solve them? Why did they decide to be detectives in the first place?

☐ Li and Andy are best friends, but they're always getting into trouble for doing crazy things. What kind of things do you think Li and Andy do? When Andy's cousin Matt comes to visit, do you think the three of them will have an adventure?

☐ Think of your own story and write about it.

Take It Further

fascinate	If something fascinates you, it interests you so much that you think about it a lot.

Cars fascinate Bobby because

perplex	If something perplexes you, it worries or confuses you because you can't figure it out.

Ronnie was perplexed about

wheeze	If someone wheezes, they have a hard time breathing and make a whistling sound when they breathe.

When Rose started to wheeze, she

sashay	Someone who sashays walks in a fancy way that they want other people to notice.

When you're wearing new shoes, you sashay down the sidewalk
so that

thwart	If something thwarts you or your plans, it stops you from getting what you want.

Britney's plans were thwarted by her mom because

distract	If something distracts you, it takes your attention away from something else.

Lisa was distracted when

squat	If you say someone or something is squat, you mean that they are short and thick.

The squat building looked like

plethora	A plethora of something is a large amount of it, sometimes more than you want or need.

Sasha had a plethora of cookies, so she

How Many Words Can I Use?

And still make sense!

☐ fascinate
☐ perplex
☐ wheeze
☐ sashay
☐ thwart
☐ distract
☐ squat
☐ plethora

Write about what you read in "Impossible Tricks." Did you try all the tricks? How did it feel when you couldn't do things like lift your own finger? Do you know any other weird things it seems like your body should be able to do, but it can't? Use as many words as you can. Have fun, but make sense!

CROSSWORD PUZZLE

word box: distracted, fascinating, sashay, wheezing, perplexed, squat, plethora, thwart

Down
1. You always stop me from doing fun things.
2. I wasn't paying attention.

Across
3. I can't breath very well.
4. You're walking in a special way—is that a new skirt?
5. I don't get it. I'm really confused.
6. Look at the short, chubby puppy!
7. That's amazing! I can't look at anything else!
8. That's a lot of marbles.

In My Own Words

Check the prompt that you want to write about. Then write a story using as many of the vocabulary words as possible. Have fun, but make sense!

☐ Write a story from the point of view of a dog. What is the dog's name? What does the dog do all day? Where does it go?

☐ Write a letter to a pen pal in South America. It can be about anything at all, true or not, just make sure it's interesting and exciting.

☐ Think of your own story and write about it.

TOTAL WORDS USED

✔ **These are the words I used!**

☐ fascinate   ☐ wheeze   ☐ thwart   ☐ squat

☐ perplex   ☐ sashay   ☐ distract   ☐ plethora

127

Take It Further

| effortless | If something you do is effortless, you do it easily and well. |

Margaret did the math homework effortlessly because

| exhibition | An exhibition is an event where either interesting things or a skillful activity is displayed. |

Harry's favorite exhibition was

| native | Someone who is a native of a particular country, state, or region was born and grew up there. |

I wish I was a native of Australia because

| coast | A vehicle that is coasting keeps going without using any power to move it. |

The boat coasted in order to

| **prowess** | Someone's prowess is their great skill at doing something. |

His prowess as a writer was shown when

| **dissuade** | If you dissuade someone from doing something, you convince them not to do it. |

My aunt dissuaded us from going to the dance by

| **bliss** | Bliss is complete happiness. |

The afternoon was full of bliss for Kristen because

| **diminutive** | If you call someone or something diminutive, you mean that they are very small. |

My little is sister is so diminutive that

How Many Words Can I Use?

And still make sense!

Write about what you read in "Interview with a Photographer." Do you like to take pictures? What do you take pictures of? Did the photographer in the interview give you any new ideas? Use as many words as you can. Have fun, but make sense!

Hidden Clues

Fill in the blanks with the vocabulary word that best fits each clue. The letters in the boxes will spell out the answer to the question at the bottom of the page. The first one has been done for you.

diminutive
effortless
bliss

coast
dissuade

prowess
exhibition
native

1. I am totally happy! This is perfect!   b l [i] s s

2. I feel like I'm two inches tall.

__ __ __ __ __ [2_] __ __ __ __

3. This bike is going really fast, and I'm not even pedaling.

__ __ __ __ [3_] __

4. You don't want to go to the carnival tonight. It won't be fun.

__ __ __ __ __ __ __ [4_]

5. You are so good at that! It's amazing.   __ [5_] __ __ __ __ __

6. I'm so glad we came. All these pictures on display are great.

[6_] __ __ __ __ __ __ __ __ __

7. They make it look so easy.

__ __ __ __ __ __ __ [7_] __

8. I was born in Texas.   __ __ [8_] __ __ __

What did Bessie Coleman use the Juneteenth celebration to do?

__ __ __ __ __ __ __ __   more people in aviation.
 1   2   3   4   5   6   7   8

In My Own Words

Check the prompt that you want to write about. Then write a story using as many of the vocabulary words as possible. Have fun, but make sense!

☐ Write a poem about the place you were born. What is unique about this place? Do you still live there? Do you want to stay where you live now? Why or why not?

☐ Sarah and her family are on a vacation at the beach. Is she happy and having fun? Why or why not? What does the family do? Who do they meet?

☐ Think of your own story and write about it.

Take It Further

| **banish** | If you banish someone from a place, you make them go away and stop them from coming back. |

Cassandra banished her little brother from her room when

| **decree** | A decree is an official order or decision made by a person or group with the authority to do it. |

The decree on the board said

| **desert** | If you desert someone or something, you leave them and stop supporting or helping them. |

The old house was deserted because

| **spare** | If you spare someone or something, you save them from being hurt or used for something else. |

Vicky spared the old magazines from being thrown away by

commend	If someone commends you, they praise you in an official way.

Nick was commended yesterday for

ruthless	Someone who is ruthless is cruel and will do anything to achieve their goals.

Jason thought his teacher was ruthless because

serene	Someone or something that is serene is calm and quiet.

For Andrea, the library is the most serene place because

covert	A covert action or thing is one that is secret or hidden.

Emilio was covert when he handed the note to Janie because

□ banish
□ decree
□ desert
□ spare
□ commend
□ ruthless
□ serene
□ covert

How Many Words Can I Use?

And still make sense!

Write about what you read in "Mole Patrol." What do you think happened at the surprise party? Was it fun? Who was there? Did Janet have a good time? Use as many words as you can. Have fun, but make sense!

Word Wiggle

Fill in the boxes around the word wiggle with the vocabulary word that best fits each clue. The first one has been done for you.

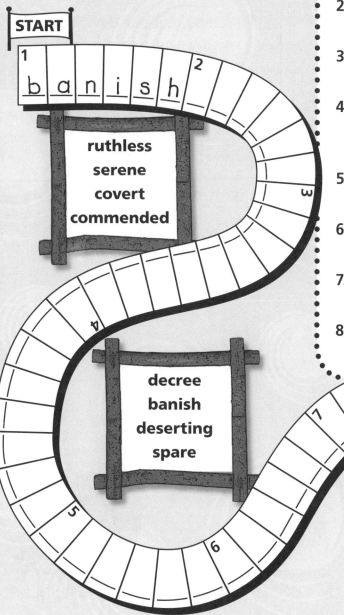

START

1. b a n i s h

ruthless
serene
covert
commended

decree
banish
deserting
spare

FINISH

1. I ___ you from my classroom! Don't come back!

2. The backyard is ___ and peaceful.

3. I'm giving up on the idea of powdered peas. I'm ___ it.

4. I'm warning you, she's ___ about making sure everyone follows the rules.

5. I, king of this land, ___ that my people will wear orange.

6. The ___ sign was a secret and it was the signal to start.

7. ___ me the lecture. I don't want to hear it!

8. The principal ___ her for her excellent attendance record.

In My Own Words

Check the prompt that you want to write about. Then write a story using as many of the vocabulary words as possible. Have fun, but make sense!

☐ Have you recently gotten rewarded for anything you've done? What was it? Did you like your reward or did you wish it had been something else? Did the attention make you happy or shy?

☐ Pretend that one day, you are sent to live in a fairy tale. Who else lives there? What is it like? How do you feel about this new place? Who sent you there and when will you come home?

☐ Think of your own story and write about it.

Take It Further

sulk	If you sulk about something, you are quiet and moody for a while because you are annoyed about it.

Rob sulked all day about

jeer	If you jeer at someone, you show you don't like them by saying mean things.

When my little sister jeered at me, I

consideration	If you give something consideration, you think about it very carefully.

Katie considered her options by

probable	If something is probable, it is likely to happen or likely to be true.

It is probable that Veronica will go to summer camp because

fumble	When you fumble for something, you clumsily try and reach for it or hold it.

Because she was wearing mittens, Lacey fumbled

for

pretentious	A pretentious person tries to seem more important than they really are.

Raul acted pretentious when he

obscure	If something is obscure, most people don't know about it or understand it.

The book was so obscure that Layla

assert	When you assert something, you say it firmly because you're very sure of it.

Jennifer asserted her beliefs when she

- [ ] **sulk**
- [ ] **jeer**
- [ ] **consideration**
- [ ] **probable**
- [ ] **fumble**
- [ ] **pretentious**
- [ ] **obscure**
- [ ] **assert**

How Many Words Can I Use?

And still make sense!

Write about what you read in "Star Light, Star... Not so Bright." Do you like to look at the stars? Pretend you threw a star gazing party for your friends last night. Who was there? What did you see? What did you do? Use as many words as you can. Have fun, but make sense!

Word Riddles

Read the clues for each number. Then fill in the blanks with the correct vocabulary word. The first one has been done for you.

1. **assert**
- This word has two vowels.
- It has to do with something you say.
- You have to know what you're talking about to do this.

2. _____
- This word has to do with how you think about something.
- This is something you do carefully.
- This word has seven consonants.

3. _____
- This word has four letters.
- This is a way to get called a "bully."
- This is a way to make fun of someone else.

4. _____
- This word has three syllables.
- This word has five consonants.
- This is another way of saying that something might happen.

5. _____
- This is something you do.
- This word has six letters.
- You can do this with a football.

6. _____
- This might happen when you're having a bad day.
- This word is a way you can act.
- This is being moody.

7. _____
- This isn't a nice word.
- This is like being snobby.
- This word has 11 letters.

8. _____
- This isn't very well known.
- This word is something people just don't understand.
- This word begins and ends with a vowel.

assert   fumble   jeer   consideration
   pretentious   obscure   sulk   probable

In My Own Words

Check the prompt that you want to write about. Then write a story using as many of the vocabulary words as possible. Have fun, but make sense!

☐ Pretend you are a newspaper writer. Write an article about an event you've been to where the crowd got upset with someone. What was it like to be there? Why were they upset?

☐ Who is the nicest person you know? Why are they so nice? Do they make other people feel good about themselves? Do you wish you were more like that person? Why?

☐ Think of your own story and write about it.

These are the words I used!

- [ ] sulk
- [ ] jeer
- [ ] consideration
- [ ] probable
- [ ] fumble
- [ ] pretentious
- [ ] obscure
- [ ] assert

TOTAL WORDS USED

Words I Have Learned

A

abandon
accolade
adversary
alibi
allure
altercation
amiable
anonymous
antic
apprehension
aroma
assail
assert
astray
astute
audacious
auspicious

B

bail
banish
bleak
bliss

C

coast
commend
compact
consideration
consistent
contender
coordination
covert
crave
crevice
crucial
cubicle

D

dainty
dazzle
decisive
decree
dedication
dejected
desert
destiny
detach
dilemma
diminutive
disband
disheveled
dissuade
distract
divine
dumbfounded
dwindle

E

effortless
eliminate
eloquent
elucidate
enigma
epidemic
escapade
evidently
excruciating
exhibition
expedition
expel
extravaganza

F

fanatical
fascinate
fathom
fatigue
feverish
fickle
flabbergasted
fleeting
foil
formative
fragment
fulfill
fumble
fume

G

gaze
glum
gratifying
grimace

H

humanitarian
hunch
hypnotic

I

impetuous
incident
incredulous
indomitable
ingenuity
insistent
intense
isolated

J

jaunt
jeer
jolt
jovial

K

keen

L

lament
levitate
lodge
lurch

M

mandate
maneuver
meander
mischief
mortify
muster

N

native
navigate
neglect
newsworthy
nonchalant
notorious

O

obscure
opponent
optimistic
outlandish
overreact

P

perplex
phenomenal
plentiful
plethora
possession
presume
pretentious
primp
probable
prospect
prosper
prowess
pry
pulverize
putrid

Q

quandary

R

radiance
rebuff
recruit
refurbish
reinforce
repulsive
reputation
resigned
resolutely
ricochet
rowdy
rummage
ruthless

S

sashay
scarcely
scoff
scrawl
scrutinize
seclusion
sedate
seldom
serene
shard
skim
sleuth
spare
speculate
squander
squat
stamina
stationary
steadfast
stifle
stupefy
suave
subtle
sulk
superior
surly

T

tactic
teem
texture
thrive
thwart
tolerate
torment
transpire
triumph

U

undeterred
unscathed

V

vanish
venture
verify
victorious
vindicate
vivacious

W

wheeze

Highlight your favorite words!

(147)

Other Favorite Words

You learn new words every day. Some of them you will always want to remember. Here is a place to write down words you learn from other places!

I

heard   saw   used

(circle one)

this word: _____.

Where and how: _____

_____

I

heard   saw   used

(circle one)

this word: _____.

Where and how: _____

_____

I

heard   saw   used

(circle one)

this word: _____.

Where and how: _____

_____

I

heard   saw   used

(circle one)

this word: _____.

Where and how: _____

_____

I

heard   saw   used

(circle one)

this word: _____.

Where and how: _____

_____

I

heard   saw   used

(circle one)

this word: _____.

Where and how: _____

_____

Word Watcher

Word Watcher

Word Watcher

Word Watcher

Word Watcher

Word Watcher